NEGATIVE AFFIRMATIONS

Thanks to:
Albert DePetrillo, Chip Stone, Frank Symons

Visit the Portrait website!

. . . .

PORTRAIT

Portrait publishes a wide range of non-fiction, including
biography, history, science, music, popular culture and sport.

Visit our website to:
- read descriptions of our popular titles
- buy our books over the internet
- take advantage of our special offers
- enter our monthly competition
- learn more about your favourite Portrait authors

VISIT OUR WEBSITE AT: www.portraitbooks.com

First published in 2006 by **Portrait**
an imprint of Piatkus Books Ltd
5 Windmill Street
London W1T 2JA
e-mail: info@piatkus.co.uk

The moral right of the author has been asserted

A catalogue record for this book is
available from the British Library

ISBN 0 7499 5118 4

Printed and bound in China by
Everbest Printing Co. Ltd

NEGATIVE AFFIRMATIONS

GEORGE MOLE & STEVEN APPLEBY

PORTRAIT

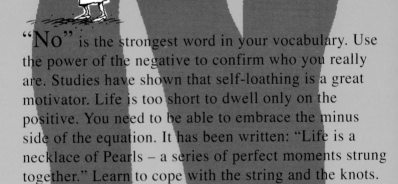

"No" is the strongest word in your vocabulary. Use the power of the negative to confirm who you really are. Studies have shown that self-loathing is a great motivator. Life is too short to dwell only on the positive. You need to be able to embrace the minus side of the equation. It has been written: "Life is a necklace of Pearls – a series of perfect moments strung together." Learn to cope with the string and the knots.

Consider easing into negativity. Try pulling away from happiness for a few days, then move to a neutral attitude for a while. After a week of this bland, noncommittal outlook, test the waters of negativism.

See yourself as others see you. Why not harness their ridicule and scorn? Why not take a few moments to make yourself the person you always feared you were? Don't waste time on dreams when you could resent yourself in the now.

Ask yourself:

"Am I ready for the Power of No?"

BASIC
AFFIRMATIONS

Speak each affirmation aloud. Now say it again.
And again. Remember, the whole point is to hammer
its message deep into your brain, so say it another 10
times. 1001 times would be even better.

In the Garden of the Spirit I am a Noxious Weed

MY LITTLE TROUBLES
ARE NOT WORTH A HILL
OF BEANS BUT I
HAVE FORGED THEM
INTO AN ALPINE
RANGE THAT CASTS
A MIGHTY SHADOW
OVER ANY HOPE OF
SALVATION

MENTALLY I MOVE THROUGH LIFE AS IF WADING THROUGH BOILED RICE

I am a snivelling, whining cur

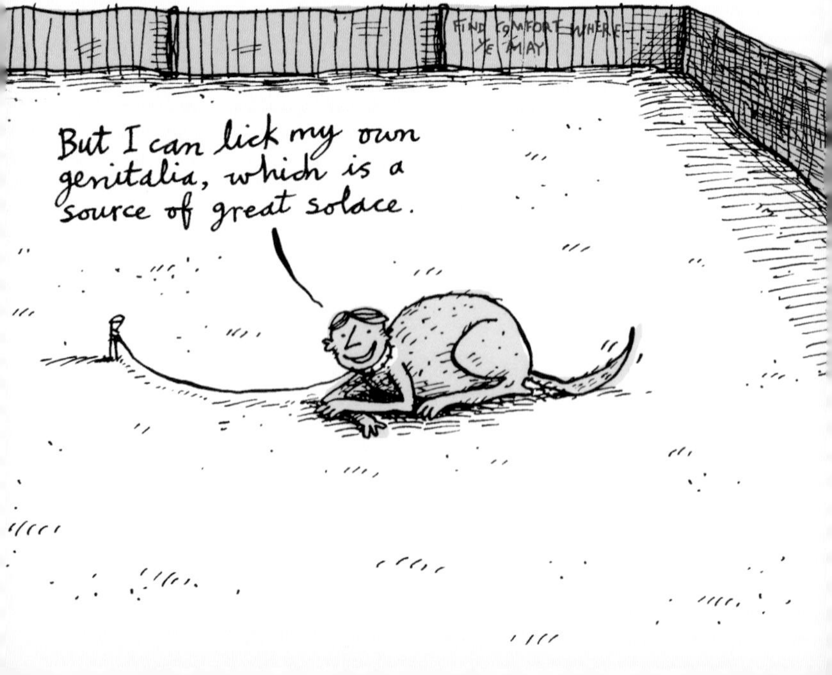

MY SEXUALITY HAS ALWAYS BEEN IN DOUBT

A LIFE OF LOVE HAS BEEN RESERVED FOR OTHERS

I AM AN

UN-PERSON

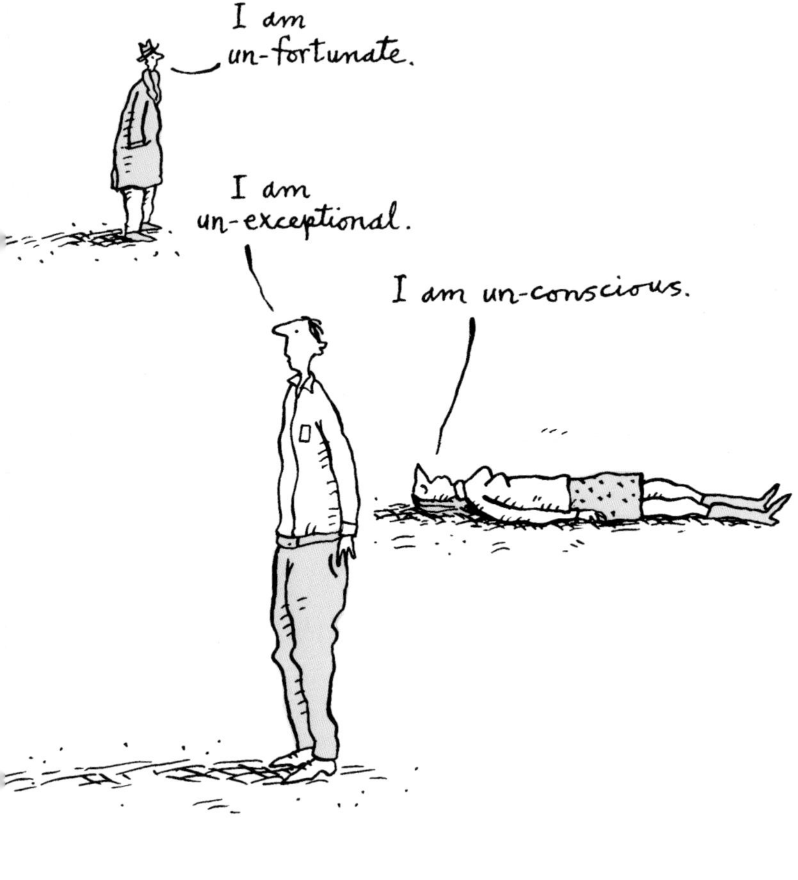

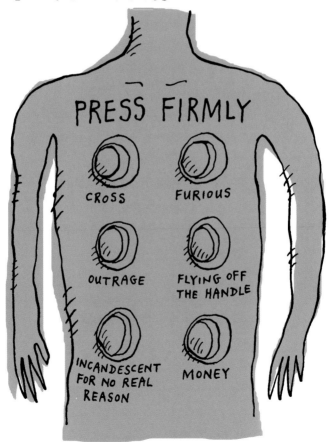

THERE IS ALWAYS DIFFICULTY

I JUST HAVE TO LOOK HARDER

LETTING
GO
MEANS
I
WILL
FALL

I AM A FLY STRUGGLING IN THE WEB OF LIFE. THE GRIM SPIDER OF FATE HAS ME IN ITS CLUTCHES AND I AM DOOMED.

MY **SHIP** CAME IN BUT NEVER **DOCKED**

THE **WINDOW** TO SUCCESS IS **SHUT**

AND **FORTUNE'S DOOR** IS **LOCKED**

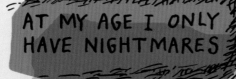

MY GREATEST ERRORS

A PRACTICAL MIND-TOOL

Before moving on to the next section, here's an exercise that will help you achieve True Negativity, including good ol' depression. List all your worst mistakes and express your moments of deepest embarrassment.

If you're having problems remembering, please use the helpful template below as an aid to releasing memories you may have been suppressing. Simply fill in the blanks.

• I remember the terrible time when I..........................

• I can't believe I .... in public.

• I don't think anyone saw me but I.................... with a ...., twice.

• I always remember the expression on her face when mother discovered me..

• Nothing would make me admit that I........................

• I have never been able to .... again after I.. with a ....

THE
CONFIRMATIONS

THOUGHTS UPON AWAKENING

The morning is a sacred time. It is when we set our agenda for the day. Take a moment to realise that although the nightmares are over the worst is yet to come.

As you resurface from the world of the unconscious, keep your eyes shut tightly for a few seconds.

Let the problems of the day crowd into your head. Listen to the cacophony they bring.

Set yourself five impossible goals, or six, or eight. The less you achieve the more frustrated you will become.

Dwell on the dissatisfaction you will feel at about 3.30 this afternoon when your blood sugar is low and you can't eat anything because you are still too full from lunch.

Now, open your eyes.

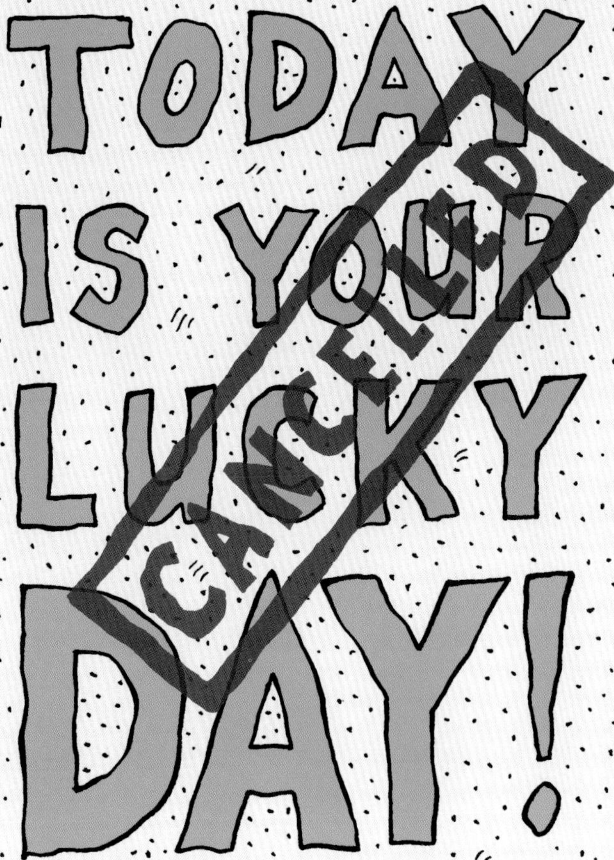
TODAY IS YOUR LUCKY DAY!
CANCELLED

YOUR GUARDIAN
ANGEL IS ON
STRIKE

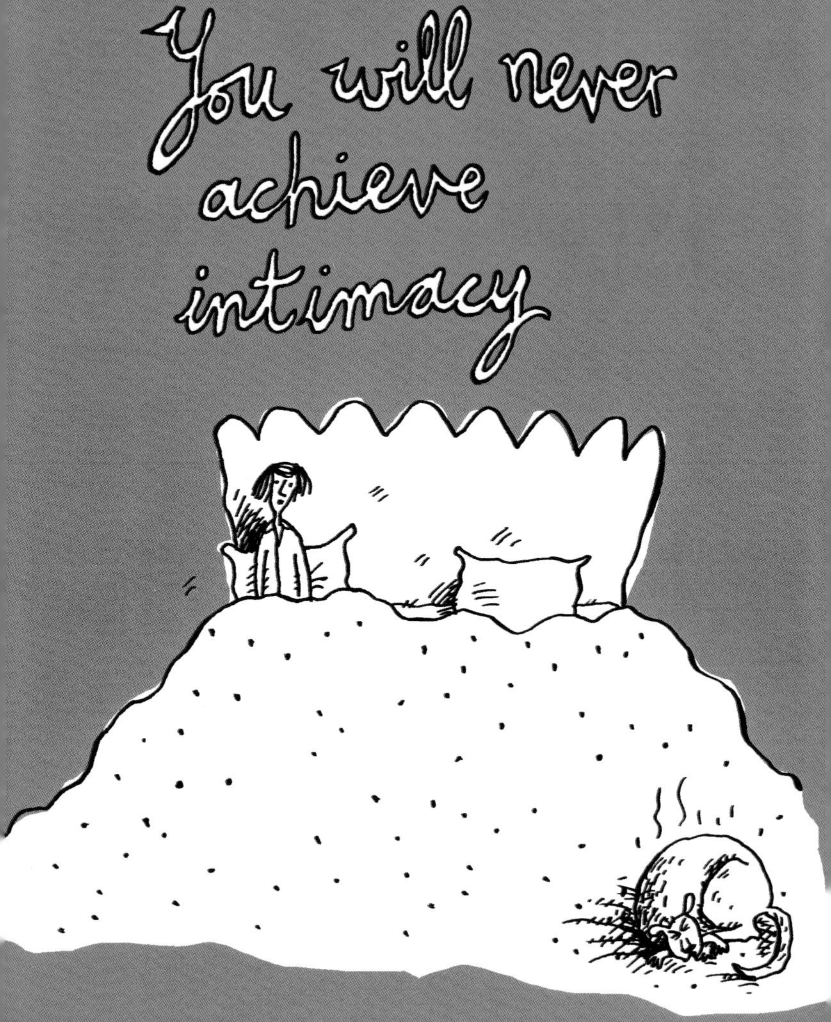
You will never achieve intimacy

YOUR

MOTHER

WAS

RIGHT!

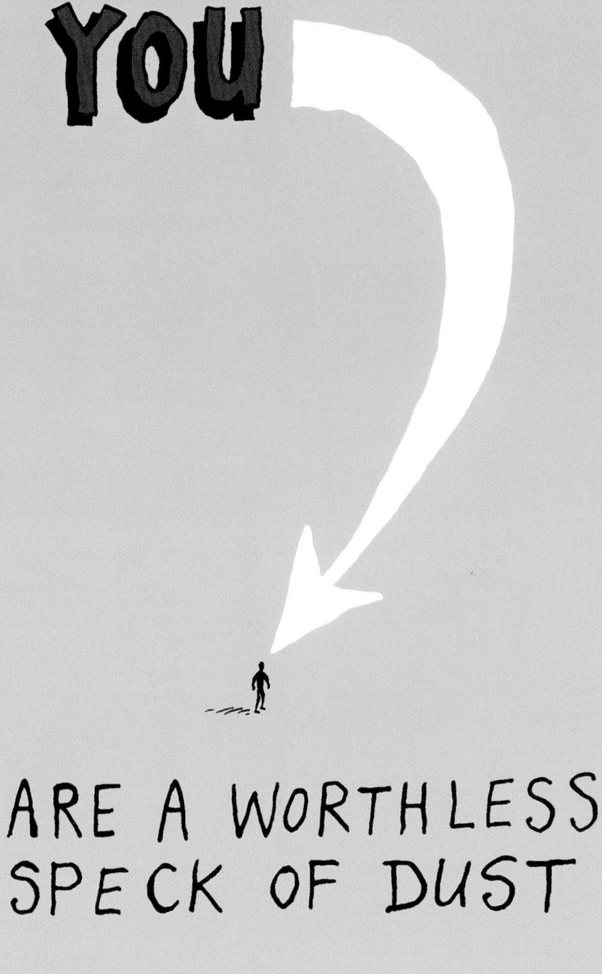
YOU
ARE A WORTHLESS
SPECK OF DUST

THE WOUNDS
OF CHILDHOOD
NEVER *HEAL*

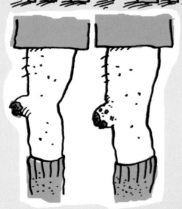

THEY JUST
SCAB OVER

ARE YOU
THINKING
AT **ALL**?!

YOU MIGHT AS
WELL WEAR A
SPOON!!

The CHILDREN are a REMINDER of my SHORTCOMINGS

VISUALISATIONS

ANOTHER GREAT MIND-TOOL!

It often helps to have an image in mind as you meditate on these affirmations and confirmations.

Take a moment for yourself. You can find an empty moment, even in the midst of your busy life.

Be creative: take a few seconds in a crowded train compartment; in a public convenience; while you wait for surgical attention; during an interminable meeting.

Close your eyes.

Visualise yourself...

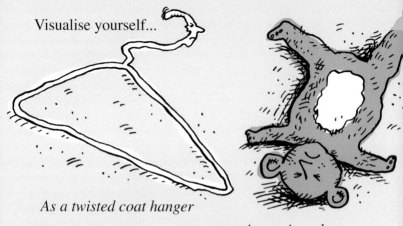

As a twisted coat hanger

As a rejected toy

As a cup of cold coffee

As an unwashed dish

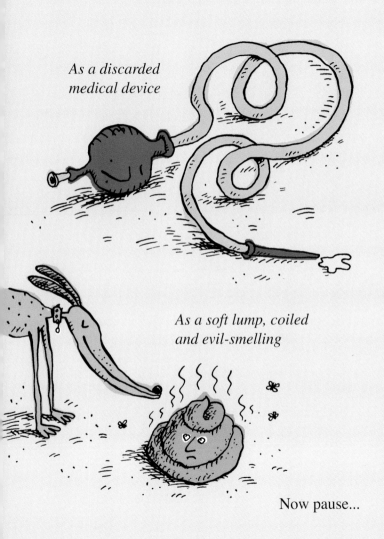

*As a discarded
medical device*

*As a soft lump, coiled
and evil-smelling*

Now pause...

Using your Third Eye *see yourself*.

Let your face express how you feel about the way you look as any one of these objects. Now open your eyes.

Are people looking at you differently? Yes, they are! This mind-tool is great for the next chapter...

NEGATIVE ADVICE

YOU ARE NOT A SHARK. YOU DO NOT NEED TO MOVE FORWARD AT ALL TIMES.

IT IS BETTER TO BE SELF-CENTRED AND FRIGID

TAKE THE TIME TO WITHHOLD AFFECTION

I RESOLVE TO PUT A FINANCIAL VALUE ON EVERYTHING*

*You can't buy
happiness
but you can
lease it and
return it when
you're bored.

APATHY

IS

A-PATH

OF

LEAST RESISTANCE

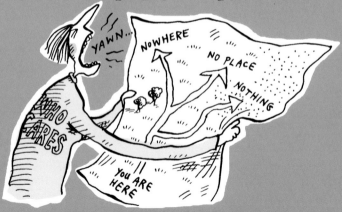

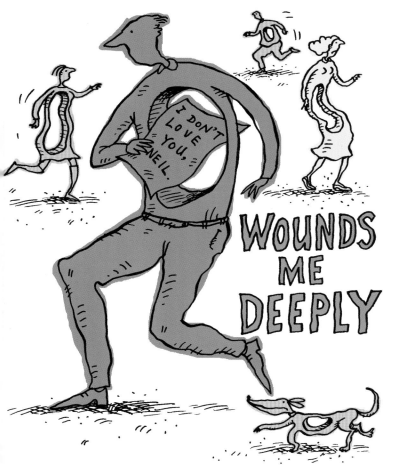

FASCISIENCE IS THE MONTIFACTOR OF BENTOVATION

Obviously...
As any fool knows.

Try very hard not to say anything of value, but if you have to say something do your best to make it incomprehensible.

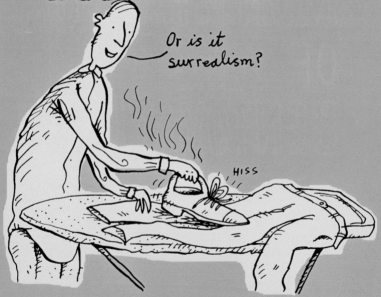

THE MIND-BODY CONNECTION

Your body is not a temple. Your body is a shack. A smoke-filled shebeen. A caravan without wheels. A dilapidated bungalow. Ask yourself: "What sect would consider worshipping in this shattered husk of flesh that imprisons my wizened wisp of a soul?"

THE MIRROR LIES

YOU **DO NOT** LOOK AS GOOD AS YOU THINK YOU DO

THE MIRROR NEVER LIES

YOU **REALLY DO** LOOK THIS BAD

FROWN

YOUR FACE NEEDS THE EXERCISE*

JUST FOLLOW THE INSTRUCTIONS BELOW:

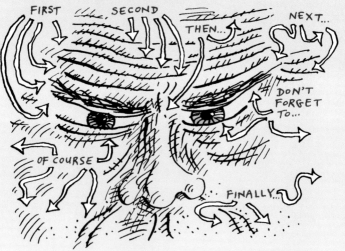

FIRST · SECOND · THEN... · NEXT... · DON'T FORGET TO... · OF COURSE · FINALLY...

*SMILING IS FOR THE LAZY. A SMILE REQUIRES FAR FEWER MUSCLES THAN A FROWN.

OVERINDULGENCE
WILL HELP ME REACH
NIRVANA

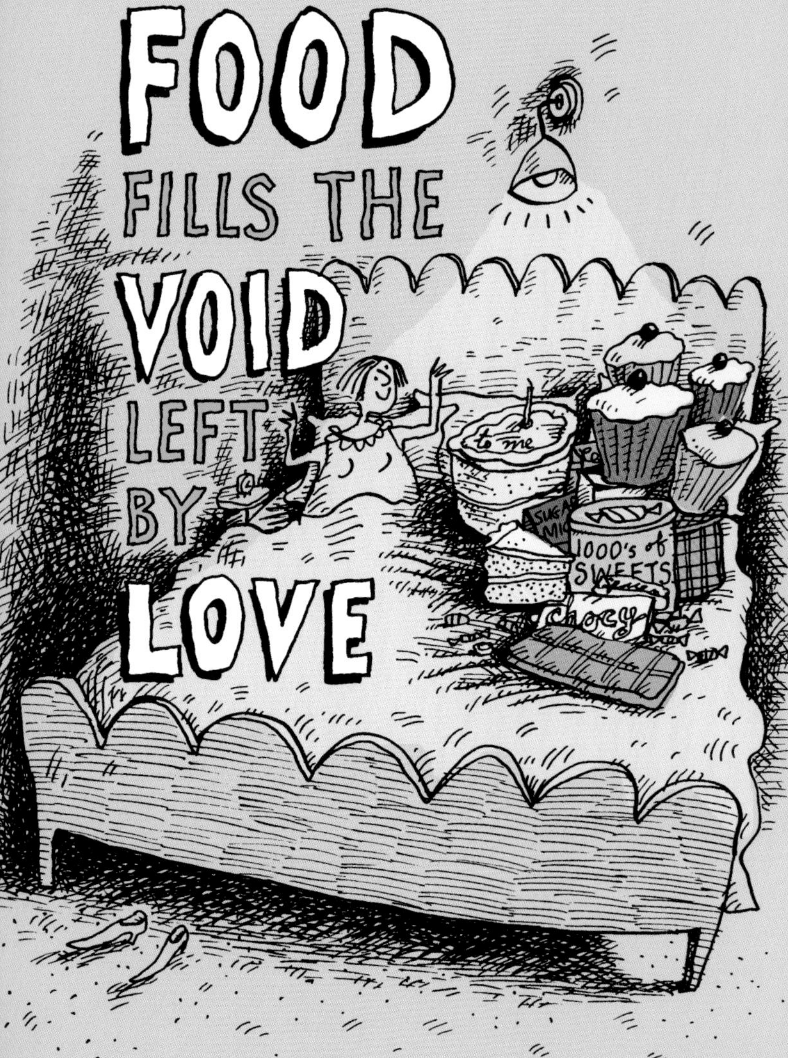
FOOD FILLS THE VOID LEFT BY LOVE
to me
1000's of SWEETS
Chocy

I AM THE FATTEST PERSON IN THE ROOM

I AM THE UGLIEST PERSON IN THE ROOM

I AM INDECISIVE. OR FAT. OR UGLY.

Or all three.
I can't
decide.

IT'S TIME TO DELVE DEEPER INTO THE MIND-BODY NEXUS...

NEGATIVE YOGA

Pose of the Chilled

Are you aware that yoga backwards plus an "n" spells "agony"? All that breathing and twisting is UN-natural and therefore the perfect way to tune your mind and turn it into a receptive vessel filled with mulch and well-rotted loam where negativity can root and thrive.

Take a look over the page at these yoga poses and ask yourself: "Do I need to be in balance this badly?"

Fish pose

Warrior pose

Mountain pose

Corpse pose

Table pose

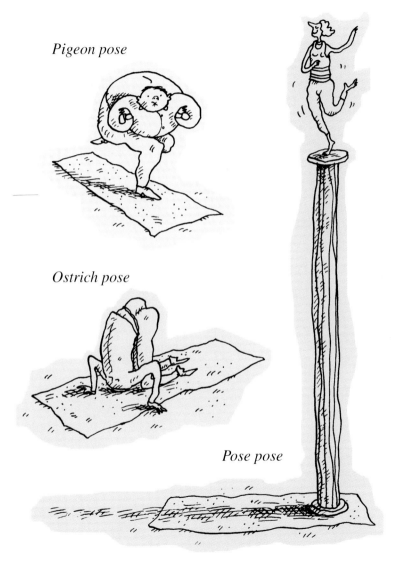

Pigeon pose

Ostrich pose

Pose pose

To enhance the efficacy of Negative Yoga why not begin your session with these

BREATHING EXERCISES

1 – Sit on the edge of an uncomfortable chair or stool.
2 – Fold your arms and cross your legs.
3 – Hunch forward slightly and allow your shoulders to tense up and rise towards your ears.
4 – Frown.
5 – Breathe 17 short, sharp, shallow breaths in through the mouth and out through the nose.

6 – Now hold your breath and count to 23.

7 – Stand up and BEND OVER. Keep holding your breath!

8 – Stand with your head as close to your legs as possible for a count of 19.

9 – Now, straighten up quickly.

You should see a few stars! With enough practice if you lengthen the counts you can probably black out instantly.

THE JOURNEY OF NO

NEGATIVITY ON THE MOVE

Staying at home narrows the mind and helps you focus on what's important. However, if you must travel, here are a few useful thoughts...

WHEN TAKING PUBLIC TRANSPORT

I am uncomfortable in the close proximity of others

The bus will never come and if it comes it will be full

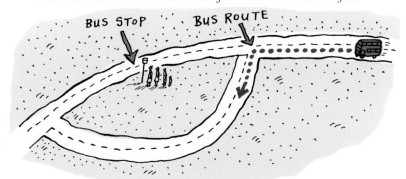

I will sleep through my stop

Snort

Typical. you wait hours then 3 ghost buses come at once!

The number 343 is a ghost bus which goes straight to hell

WHEN TRAVELLING BY PRIVATE CAR

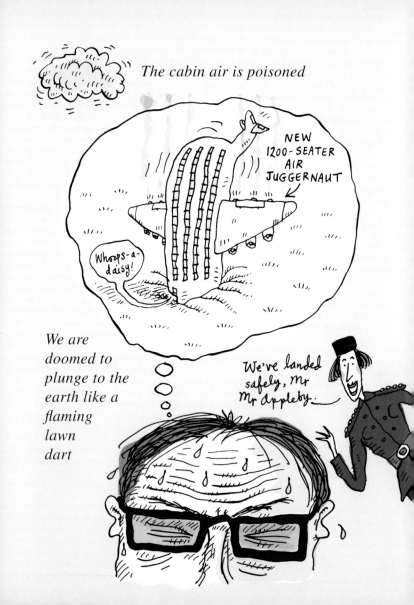

You have almost finished this book.

We suggest that you carry the book with you at all times so you can Consult the Negative on a daily basis and Top Up your Negativity at short notice.

A FINAL THOUGHT...

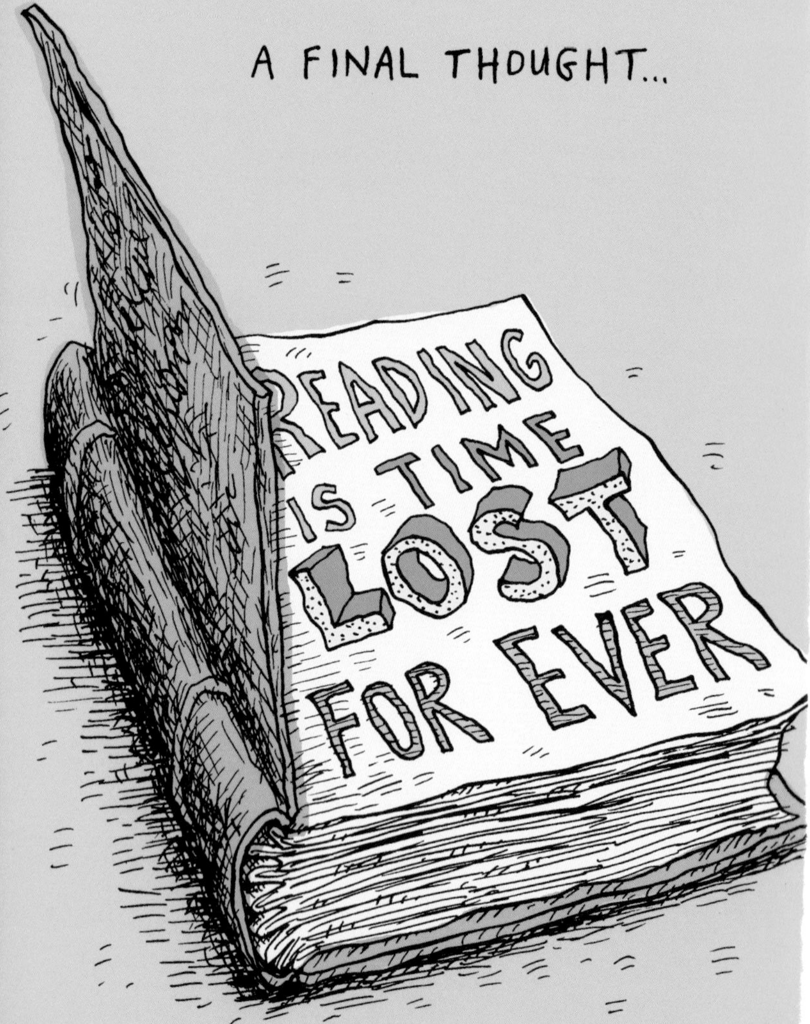